Junior Guide to
FRENCH

Annabel Warrender
and Sophie Brudenell-Bruce

Illustrated by Joseph McEwan

Designed by Graham Round
Edited by Jenny Tyler

Contents

3 How to Use this Book
4 Pronunciation Guide
5 Some Basic Words and Phrases
6 Finding Your Way
8 At the Railway Station
10 Travelling by Car
12 At the Hotel
14 Going Camping
16 Going Shopping
18 The Shops 1
20 The Shops 2
22 Posting a Letter . . . and Changing Money
24 Going to a Café
26 Going to a Restaurant
28 The Menu
30 Entertainments 1
32 Entertainments 2
33 Sightseeing 1
34 Sightseeing 2
36 Making Friends
38 Playing Games
40 Sports
42 At the Seaside 1
44 At the Seaside 2
46 Accidents and Emergencies
48 Using the Telephone
50 Feeling Ill
52 Parts of the Body
53 Colours
54 Months, Seasons, Days
56 The Weather
57 Numbers
58 The Time
60 Basic Grammar
62 Index

First published in 1979 by
Usborne Publishing Ltd.
20 Garrick Street. London WC2E 9BJ.
England.
Printed in Belgium.

How to Use this Book

This book will help you make yourself understood in most everyday situations when you are on holiday or travelling in France. The phrases have been kept as simple as possible, and include some of the possible answers to the questions you may want to ask. There are also translations of many of the signs you will see.

The book is divided into sections, each covering a situation you are likely to find yourself in. Use the contents list at the front or the index at the back to help you find the pages you need. You will find it easier if you look up the section you are going to need in advance, so you can practise saying the phrases.

For most phrases, there is a picture with a speech bubble containing the French. Underneath the picture is a guide to help you pronounce the French and an English translation. Like this:

Je parle français.

Jer parl fronsay.
I can speak French.

On the next two pages, you will find out how to use the pronunciation guide and there are some useful hints and phrases to remember. At the back of the book, there are a few common verbs and some very basic French grammar.

Points to remember

We have not always had enough space to include the words for "please" (*s'il vous plaît*). Try to remember to add them when you are asking for things.

S'il vous plaît

There are two words in French for "you" — *vous* and *tu*. *Tu* is used by close friends and children. Be careful about using *tu*, because people will think you rude if you say it to someone you don't know very well. We have used *vous* in this book, except where the conversation is between children as, for instance, in the section on "Making Friends".

Tu or Vous?

Pronunciation Guide

We have tried to keep the pronunciation guides in this book as simple as possible. For each French sound, we have used the English word, or part of a word, which sounds most like it. Read the pronunciation guide in what seems to be the most obvious way and try not to stress one syllable more than another. It will sound better if you say it quickly, so it is a good idea to practise a bit. People should be able to understand what you are saying, even if you won't sound quite like a French person. If you want to learn really good pronunciation you should try to find a French person to teach you..

Here are some general points to remember when you are trying to speak French.

The French "j" has a soft sound, like the sound in the middle of the English word "leisure". Whenever you see a "j" in the pronunciation guide you should say it in this way.

Many French words have a "nasal" ("nose-y") sound which we do not have in English. We have used "ong" and "ang" for this in the pronunciation guide.

When you are saying this, do not stress the "g". It should almost not be there.

The French "r" should be rolled at the back of the throat, rather like the sound you make when you gargle. See if you can do it. If you can't, don't worry, people will still be able to understand you.

In French, "h" is silent, so when you see one in a French word just ignore it.

Consonants (that is, all letters except a, e, i, o and u) at the ends of words are not usually pronounced, as in *l'aéroport* (airport), which is pronounced lairo-por.

You will see four different kinds of accents when you are reading French words. An "e" at the end of the word is not pronounced unless it has an acute accent on top, like this, "é". Then you pronounce it as "ay"

The French "u" is pronounced like the "ew" in the English word "dew". We have used "ew" for it in the pronunciation guide. For example:

allumettes (matches)
= allewmett

Some Basic Words and Phrases

Here are some useful words and phrases which you will need in all kinds of situations.

Oui
Wee
Yes

Non
Nong
No

S'il vous plaît
Seelvooplay
Please

Merci
Mairsee
Thank you

Bonjour
Bongjoor
Hello

Au revoir
Orvwar
Goodbye

Pardon
Pardong
I'm sorry

Excusez-moi
Exkewzay-mwah
Excuse me

Monsieur
Moosyer
Mr

Madame
Madarm
Mrs

Mademoiselle
Madmwazell
Miss

Some simple questions

How much or many?	Combien? Combeeyen?
Why?	Pourquoi? Poorkwah?
Which one?	Lequel or Laquelle? Lerkell or lahkell?
Where is...?	Où est...? Oo ay...?
When?	Quand? Kong?
Have you...?	Avez-vous...? Avay-voo...?
Is or are there...?	Y a-t-il...? Ee ateel...?

Some simple statements

I am	Je suis... Jer swee...
I have...	J'ai... Jay...
It is...	C'est... Say...
It is here.	C'est ici. Set ee-see.
It is there.	C'est là. Say lah.
Over there.	Là-bas Lah-bah
This one	Celui-ci Sirlwee-see
That one	Celui-là Sirlwee-lah
I would like...	Je voudrais.. Jer voodray..

Problems with the language

Do you speak English?
Parlez-vous anglais?
Parlay-voo ong-glay?

I do not speak French.
Je ne parle pas français.
Jer ner parl pah fronsay.

I do not understand.
Je ne comprends pas.
Jer ner comprong pah.

Please speak more slowly.
Plus lentement, s'il vous plaît.
Plew lonte-mong, seelvooplay.

What does that mean?
Qu'est-ce que cela veut dire?
Kessker sirlah ver deer?

Finding Your Way

Pour la gare, s'il vous plaît?

Poor lah gahr, seelvooplay?
How do I get to the railway station, please?

Il faut prendre l'autobus numéro 6.

Eel foe prondr lohtohbewss newmairoh seess.
You must take a number 6 bus.

Où est l'arrêt de l'autobus pour Versailles?

Là-bas. C'est celui-là.

Oo ay larray der lohtohbewss poor Vairsigh?
Where is the bus-stop for Versailles?

Lah bah. Say sirlwee lah.
Over there. It's that one.

Dois-je descendre ici pour Versailles?

Dwarj dessondr ee-see poor Vairsigh?
Is this where I get off for Versailles?

Où est le château, s'il vous plaît?

Oo ay ler shattoh, seelvooplay?
Where is the castle, please?

Je suis perdu. Quel est le nom de cette rue?

Jer swee pairdew. Kell ay ler nom der set rew?
I'm lost. What is the name of this street?

Pouvez-vous me la montrer sur le plan?

Poovay voo mer lah montray syoor ler plong?
Can you show me on the map.

General directions

Tournez à droite.
Toornay ah drwut.
Turn right.

Tournez à gauche.
Toornay ah goash.
Turn left.

Continuez tout droit.
Conteenew-ay too drwuh.
Go straight on.

 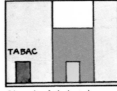 

C'est en face du cinéma.
Set ong fass dew
seenaymah.
**It's opposite the
cinema.**

C'est à côté du tabac.
Set ah coatay dew
tabah.
**It's next to the
tobacconists.**

C'est au coin de la rue.
Set oh cwang der lah rew.
It's on the corner.

 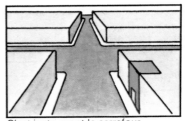

C'est juste après le pont.
Say joost appray ler pong.
It's just after the bridge.

C'est juste avant le carrefour.
Say joost avong ler carrfoor.
It's just before the crossroads.

Some places to ask for

la gare
lah gahr
railway station.

l'aéroport
lairohpor
airport

la gendarmerie
lah jondarmeree
police station

la banque
lah bonk
bank

les magasins
lay magazang
the shops

At the Railway Station

Où est-ce qu'on achète les billets ?

Là-bas, au guichet.

Oo esskon ashett lay beeyay ?
Where can I buy a ticket ?

Lah bah, oh geeshay.
Over there, at the ticket office.

C'est combien pour Paris ?

Un billet simple pour Paris.

Deux billets aller-retour pour Paris.

Say combeeyen poor Paree?
How much is it to Paris ?

Urn beeyay sampl poor Paree.
One single ticket to Paris.

Durr beeyay allay-retoor poor Paree.
Two return tickets to Paris.

De quel quai part le train pour Paris ?

Quai numéro 5.

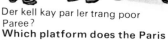

Der kell kay par ler trang poor Paree?
Which platform does the Paris train leave from ?

Kay newmairoh sank.
Platform 5.

A quelle heure part le train ?

Ah kell urr par ler trang ?
What time does the train leave ?

Say beeyen ler trang poor Paree?
Is this the Paris train?

Jay pairdew mong beeyay!
I've lost my ticket!

Ah kell urr arreev ler trang der Callay?
What time does the train from Calais arrive?

Porturr!
Porter!

Information

Luggage collection

Waiting room

Lost property

Train departures

Main line trains

District line trains

Left luggage

Not drinking water

Do not lean out of the window

Travelling by Car

Où est le garage le plus proche?

Oo ay ler gararj ler plew prosh?
Where is the nearest garage?

Combien d'essence voulez-vous?

Combeeyen dessonss voolay voo?
How much petrol do you want?

Le plein, s'il vous plaît.

Ler plan, seelvooplay.
Fill it up please.

Pouvez-vous vérifier l'huile et l'eau?

Poovay voo vayreefeeyay lweel ay low?
Can you check the oil and the water?

Je suis en panne.

Jer sweez ong pann.
I have broken down.

Qu'est-ce qui ne va pas?

Kesskee ner vah pah?
What's the trouble?

Les freins ne marchent pas bien.

Lay fran ner marshong pas beeyen.
The brakes are not working properly.

VOITURES DE LOCATION

Je voudrais louer une voiture pour la semaine, s'il vous plaît.

Jer voodray loo-ay ewn vwut-yoor poor lah sirmen, seelvooplay.
I would like to hire a car for the week, please.

Parts of the car

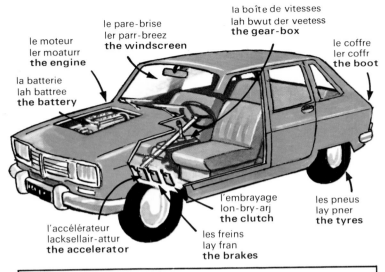

le moteur
ler moaturr
the engine

la batterie
lah battree
the battery

le pare-brise
ler parr-breez
the windscreen

la boîte de vitesses
lah bwut der veetess
the gear-box

le coffre
ler coffr
the boot

l'embrayage
lon-bry-arj
the clutch

les pneus
lay pner
the tyres

l'accélérateur
lacksellair-attur
the accelerator

les freins
lay fran
the brakes

Road signs

Found in forests and dry areas. Warns of the danger of fire.

You have the right of way over cars coming in from side roads.

You no longer have the right of way.

Restricted parking area. Must have a permit, or "Disque Bleue".

Motorway toll 1,000m away.

Entrance to car-park.

Means all through traffic should go this way.

Town centre this way.

Speed limit and end of speed limit signs. Don't forget the numbers are in kilometres.

At the Hotel

A list of recommended hotels and their prices can be obtained from the local tourist office *(Syndicat d'Initiative)*. When staying overnight, you must register with the police. The hotel will usually keep your passport a short while and do this for you.

Booking in advance

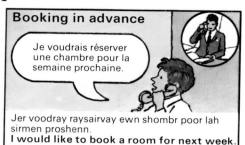

Je voudrais réserver une chambre pour la semaine prochaine.

Jer voodray raysairvay ewn shombr poor lah sirmen proshenn.
I would like to book a room for next week.

Finding a room

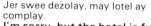

Je suis désolé, mais l'hôtel est complet.

Jer swee dezolay, may lotel ay complay.
I'm sorry, but the hotel is full.

Est-ce que vous pouvez me conseiller un autre hôtel ?

Essker voo poovay mer consayay urn ohtr otel ?
Can you recommend another hotel ?

Une chambre à deux lits.

Ewn shombr ah durr lee.
A room with two beds.

Une chambre pour deux personnes, avec salle de bain.

Ewn shombr poor durr pairsonn aveck sall der bang.
A double room with bathroom.

Une chambre pour une personne avec douche.

Ewn shombr poor ewn pairson aveck doosh.
A single room with shower.

Vous comptez rester combien de temps ?

Voo contay restay combeeyen der tong ?
How long will you be staying ?

Hotel meals

TARIF

Chambre avec petit déjeuner
Bed and breakfast

Demi-pension
Half board

Pension complète
Full board

A quelle heure servez-vous le petit déjeuner (déjeuner, dîner) ?

Ah kell urr sairvay-voo ler pertee dayjernay (dayjernay, deenay) ?
What time is breakfast (lunch, dinner) served ?

Oeuf sur le plat
Urf syoor ler plah
Fried egg

Oeuf à la coque
Urf ah lah cock
Boiled egg

Oeufs brouillés
Urf breweeyay
Scrambled eggs

Croissant
Cwassong
Flaky roll

Pourriez-vous me faire un pique-nique ?

Pooreeyay voo mer fair urn peek-neek ?
Could you make me a packed lunch ?

Ma clef, s'il vous plaît.

Quel est le numéro de votre chambre ?

Mah clay, seal voo play.
My key, please.

Kell ay ler newmairoh der vottr shombr ?
What is your room number ?

Je voudrais laisser un message pour mon frère.

Jer voodray laysay urn messarj poor mon frair.
I would like to leave a message for my brother.

Paying the bill

Voulez-vous me préparer la note, s'il vous plaît ?

Voolay-voo mer preparay lah nott seal voo play ?
My bill, please.

13

Going Camping

Campsites are graded and given from one to four stars. The four star camps are highly organized with many facilities. You can hire caravans, tents or chalets at some camps. You should book in advance if you will be camping during July or August.

Finding a campsite

Peut-on camper ici?

Pert-ong compay ee-see?
May we camp here?

Est-ce qu'il y a un terrain de camping près d'ici?

Esskeel ya urn terang der comping pray dee-see?
Is there a campsite near here?

Nous avons une caravane et deux tentes.

Noozavong ewn caravan ay durr taunt.
We have a caravan and two tents.

At the campsite

Nous voudrions rester quinze jours.

Noo voodreeong restay kanz joor.
We would like to stay a fortnight.

Avez-vous un endroit plus ombragé?

Avay voo urn ondrwah plooz ombrarjay?
Have you a shadier place?

Y a-t-il d'autres familles anglaises ici?

Ee ateel doetr fameey ong-glairz ee-see?
Are there any other English families here?

A quelle heure fermez-vous le soir?

Ah kell urr fairmay voo ler swar?
What time do you close in the evenings?

Ooessker jer per mer lavay ?
Where can I wash ?

Oo essker jer per troovay de low ?
Where can I find some water ?

Essker jer per omprantay vottr lomp der posh ?
May I borrow your torch ?

Essker say pairmee der fair urn fur der comp ?
Are we allowed to make a camp fire ?

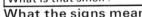

Kell ay set ohdurr ?
What is that smell ?

Pooreeyay voo fair urn per mwan der brwee, sealvooplay ?
Please could you make less noise ?

What the signs mean

DÉFENSE DE LAVER LA VAISSELLE DANS LES LAVABOS.
No washing up in the basins.

PARKING OBLIGATOIRE
Compulsory parking

EAU POTABLE
Drinking water

RESERVÉ AUX CARAVANES
Caravans only

MESSIEURS LES CAMPEURS SONT PRIÉS DE DÉPOSER LEURS ORDURES DANS LES ENDROITS PRÉVUS À CET EFFET.
Campers are requested to dispose of their rubbish in the places provided.

Going Shopping

Shops are generally open from 8.00 a.m. to 7.00 p.m. Most close on Sundays and many also on Mondays. On the next pages, you can find out where to buy different things. Remember that metric weights and measures are used.

Oo pweej ashtay day frwee?
Where can I buy some fruit?

Avay-voo day pomm?
Have you any apples?

Combeeyen ong voodreeay-voo?
How many would you like?

Urn keelo.
A kilo.

Kattr tronsh der jombong, sealvooplay.
Four slices of ham, please.

Jer regard sirlmong.
I am just looking.

Signs

Sale

ASCENSEUR

Lifts

Libre Service

Self Service

Ouvert de 9h à 18.30h

Open from 9 a.m. to 6.30 p.m.

Buying clothes

Pouvez-vous m'aider? Je cherche une chemise imprimée.

Poovay-voo mayday? Jer shairsh ewn shermeez ampreemay.
Can you help me? I am looking for a patterned shirt.

Oui. Quelle taille voulez-vous?

Wee. Kell tye voolay-voo?
Yes. What size do you want?

Puis-je l'essayer?

Pweej lessayay?
May I try it on?

C'est trop grand.
Say troh grong.
It's too big.

C'est trop petit.
Say troh pertee.
It's too small.

C'est trop large.
Say troh larj.
It's too loose.

C'est trop serré.
Say troh serray.
It's too tight.

Ça fait combien?

Sa fay combeeyen?
How much is it?

Avez-vous quelque chose de moins cher?

Avay-voo kellker showz der mwang shair?
Have you anything cheaper?

Où dois-je payer?

Oo dwarj payay?
Where should I pay?

Merci.

Je vous en prie.

Mairsee.
Thank you.

Jer vooz ong pree.
You are welcome.

The Shops 1

Je voudrais . . .

Jer voodray . . .
I would like . . .

des conserves
day konsairv
some tinned foods

du fromage
dew fromarj
some cheese

du beurre
dew burr
some butter

des œufs
dez ur
some eggs

de la confiture
der lah konfeetyoor
some jam

du thé
dew tay
some tea

du sucre
dew syookr
some sugar

des biscuits
day bee-skwee
biscuits

du lait
dew lay
some milk

du miel
dew mee-el
some honey

de la moutarde
der lah mootard
some mustard

du café
dew caffay
some coffee

des haricots verts
dez arreecoe vair
some green beans

des petits pois
day pertee pwah
some peas

un chou-fleur
urn shoo-flurr
a cauliflower

des pommes de terre
day pomm der tair
some potatoes

une laitue
ewn laytew
a lettuce

des champignons
day shompeenyon
some mushrooms

un chou
urn shoo
a cabbage

des tomates
day tomart
some tomatoes

des oignons
dez oy-nyong
some onions

des framboises
day frombwarz
some raspberries

des pommes
day pomm
some apples

des poires
day pwar
some pears

une orange
ewn oranj
an orange

un citron
urn seetrong
a lemon

des fraises
day frairz
some strawberries

des reines-claudes
day renn-clode
some greengages

des prunes
day proon
some plums

18

BOUCHERIE

Boosheree
Butcher

du hachis de bœuf
dew ashee der berf
some minced beef

un poulet
urn poolay
a chicken

un bifteck
urn beefteck
a steak

des escalopes de veau
dez escallopp der voe
some veal escalopes

des côtelettes d'agneau
day cottlett da-nyoh
some lamb chops

Charcuterie

Sharkewtree
Pork Butcher

des côtelettes de porc
day cottlett der porr
some pork chops

des saucisses
day sohseess
some sausages

du pâté
dew pattay
some paté

du saucisson
dew sohseesong
some salami

des hors-d'oeuvres
dez orr durrvr
**some prepared salads
and cooked meats**

BOULANGERIE

Boolonjeree
Baker

des brioches
day breeosh
some sweet rolls

du pain
dew pang
some bread

une baguette
ewn bagett
a long, thin loaf

PATISSERIE-CONFISERIE
Pateeseree-Konfeeseree
Cake and Sweet Shop

une tarte aux fruits
ewn tart oh frwee
a fruit tart

un gâteau
urn gattoh
a cake

des bonbons
day bongbong
some sweets

POISSONNERIE

Pwussonneree
Fishmonger

une sole
ewn soal
a sole

des crevettes
day krevett
some prawns

un poisson de la région
urn pwahsonn der lah ray-jeeong
a local kind of fish

du cabillaud
dew kabee-yoh
some cod

The Shops 2

Librairie·Papeterie·Maison de la Presse
Leebrairee-Papeeteree-Mayzong der lah Press
Bookshop-Stationers-Newspaper Shop

de l'encre
der lonckr
some ink

un stylo
urn steelo
a pen

un livre
urn leevr
a book

du papier à lettres
dew papeeyay ah lettr
some writing paper

une gomme
ewn gomm
a rubber

un crayon
urn crayong
a pencil

un journal
urn joor-nal
a newspaper

TABAC
Tabah
Tobacconist

des enveloppes
dez onvelopp
some envelopes

un briquet
urn breekay
a lighter

un paquet de cigarettes
urn packay der seegarett
a packet of cigarettes

des allumettes
des allewmett
some matches

des timbres
day tamb
some stamps

boutique de vêtements
Booteek der Vettmong
Clothes Shop

un short
urn short
some shorts

un chapeau
urn shappoh
a hat

une chemise
ewn shermeez
a shirt

une jupe
ewn jyoop
a skirt

une robe
ewn robb
a dress

des chaussures
day showsyoor
some shoes

des sandales
day sondarl
some sandals

un pull-over
urn poolovair
a jersey

un maillot de bain
urn my-oh der bang
a bathing costume

un imperméable
urn ampairmay-arbl
a raincoat

un pantalon
urn pontalong
some trousers

des collants
day collong
some tights

QUINCAILLERIE · DROGUERIE

Kye-n-kye-eree-Drogree
Ironmongers-Hardware Store

un ouvre-boîtes
urn oovr-bwut
a tin opener

une lampe de poche
ewn lomp der posh
a torch

un tournevis
urn toornvees
a screwdriver

un tire-bouchon
urn teer-booshong
a corkscrew

une pile
ewn peel
a battery

une ampoule
ewn ompool
a light bulb

de la ficelle
der lah feessell
some string

de la lessive
der lah lesseev
some detergent

des ciseaux
day seezoh
some scissors

du coton
dew cotong
some cotton

une aiguille
ewn aygwee
a needle

une prise
ewn preese
a plug

du gaz de camping
dew gaz der compeeng
some Camping Gas

Pharmacie

Farmassee **Chemist**

de l'insecticide
der lanseck-tee-seed
some insect repellent

du savon
dew savong
some soap

de l'aspirine
der laspee-reen
some aspirin

une bande
ewn bond
a bandage

de la crème antiseptique
der lah crem anteesepteek
some antiseptic cream

du talc
dew talk
some talcum powder

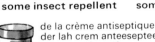
du dentifrice
dew donteefreess
some toothpaste

une brosse à dents
ewn bross ah dong
a toothbrush

des sparadraps
day sparadrah
some sticking plasters

un peigne
urn penn
a comb

du papier hygiénique
dew papeeyay eejee-ayneek
some toilet paper

une pellicule
ewn pelleckewl
a film

Posting a Letter . . .

The post office is called the P. & T. *(Postes et Téléphones)*. They are usually open from 8.00 a.m. to 7.00 p.m. on weekdays, and from 8.00 a.m. to midday on Saturdays. Stamps can also be bought from a *café-tabac*. Post boxes are usually yellow.

Quel est le prix d'un timbre pour une carte postale pour l'Angleterre?

Kelly ay ler pree durn tambr poor ewn cart postarl poor long-gletair?

How much is a stamp for a postcard to England?

Je voudrais quatre timbres pour l'Angleterre.

Jer voodray kattr tambr poor long-gletair.

I would like four stamps for England.

Où puis-je trouver une boîte aux lettres?

Oo pweej troovay ewn bwut oh lettr?

Where can I find a postbox?

The post office

Où est le bureau principal des P. & T. s'il vous plaît?

Oo ay ler bewroh pranseepal day Pay ay Tay, sealvooplay?

Where is the main post office, please?

TÉLÉGRAMMES

Je voudrais envoyer un télégramme en Angleterre.

Jer voodray onvwye-ay urn taylaygram on ong-gletair.

I would like to send a telegram to England.

Remplissez cette fiche, s'il vous plaît.

Rompleesay set feesh, sealvooplay.

Fill in this form please.

Quel est le prix par mot?

Kell ay ler pree par mow?

How much is it per word?

...and Changing Money

Ça coûte combien pour envoyer ce paquet à l'Angleterre?

Sah coot combeeyun poor on-vwyeay sir packay ah long-gletair?
How much will it cost to send this parcel to England?

A quelle heure a lieu la dernière levée de courrier?

Ah kell urr ah lyer lah dairnee-air lervay der cooree-ay?
What time does the last post leave?

Signs

TÉLÉGRAMMES

Telegrams

TIMBRES POSTE

Postage stamps

PAR AVION

Air mail

PAQUETS

Parcels

JETONS

Telephone tokens

Changing money

Traveller's cheques can be changed in a bank, a *Bureau de Change* or in some officially authorized hotels. Banks are open from 9.00 a.m. to midday and from 2.00 p.m. to 4.30 p.m. In country areas they may open on only a few days.

Puis-je encaisser un chèque de voyage ici?

Pweej onkessay urn sheck der vwye-arj ee-see?
Can I cash a traveller's cheque here?

Combien vaut la livre?

Combeeyen voh lah leevr?
How many francs are there to the pound?

Pourriez-vous me donner de la monnaie?

Pooree-ay voo mer donnay der lah monnay?
Could I have some small change?

Going to a Café

Cafés stay open from early in the morning to very late at night. They serve snack meals and both alcoholic and non-alcoholic drinks. It is cheaper if you stand inside at the bar than if you sit at a table. Many cafés have pinball machines inside.

Est-ce que cette table est occupée?

Essker set tarbl ett ockewpay?
Is this table taken?

Qu'est-ce que je vous sers, Messieurs?

Kessker jer voo sair, Messyer?
What can I get you?

Je voudrais voir la carte, s'il vous plaît.

Jer voodray vwar lah cart, seelvoo-play.
I would like to see the menu, please.

Qu'est-ce que vous avez comme sandwichs?

Jambon, fromage et saucisson.

Kessker vooz avay comm sondweech?
What sandwiches have you got?
Jombong, fromarj ay sohseesong.
Ham, cheese and salami.

Je voudrais deux sandwichs au jambon, un Coca et une orange pressée.

Jer voodray durr sondweech oh jombong, urn Coca ay ewn oronj pressay.
I would like two ham sandwiches, a Coca-Cola and an orange juice.

24

Une fourchette, s'il vous plaît.

Ewn foorshet, seelvooplay.
A fork, please.

Some things you might need to ask for

un couteau
urn kootoh
a knife

une carafe d'eau
ewn caraf doe
a jug of water

Ce n'est pas ce que j'ai commandé.

Sir nay pah sir ker jay commonday.
This is not what I ordered.

une cuiller
ewn kwee-air
a spoon

un verre
urn vair
a glass

une serviette
ewn sairvee-ett
a napkin

le sel et le poivre
ler sell ay ler pwarvr
salt and pepper

Où sont les toilettes?

Oo song lay twullett?
Where is the toilet?

Monsieur!

Moosyer!
Waiter!

L'addition, s'il vous plaît.

Ladeesseeong, seelvooplay.
The bill, please.

Est-ce que le service est compris?

Essker ler sairveess ay compree?
Is service included?

Going to a Restaurant

Restaurants usually display the menu in the window outside. Look out for restaurants with a sign saying *Relais Routiers*. In these you can get a good meal at a very reasonable price. A *brasserie* is a cheap restaurant which serves draught beer and simple meals.

Booking a table

Je voudrais réserver une table pour quatre à 20 heures.

Jer voodray rayzairvay ewn tarbl poor kattr ah vant urr.
I would like to book a table for four at 8 p.m.

Avez-vous une table pour quatre?

Avay-voozewn tarbl poor kattr?
Have you a table for four?

Avez-vous réservé?

Avay-voo rayzairvay?
Have you booked?

Avez-vous une table dans le jardin?

Avay-vooz ewn tarbl dong ler jardang?
Have you a table in the garden?

Etes-vous prêt à commander?

Ett-voo pret ah commonday?
Are you ready to order?

Comment préparez-vous ce plat?

Commong prayparay-voo sir plah?
How is this dish cooked?

Avez-vous quelque chose de très simple?

Avay-voo kellker showz der tray sampl?
Have you got anything very plain?

Drinks

Est-ce que je pourrais voir la carte des vins ?

Essker jer pooray vwar lah cart day vang?
Could I see the wine list?

Qu'est-ce que vous me recommandez ?

Kessker voo mer recommonday?
What do you recommend?

Je voudrais une carafe de vin ordinaire, et une bouteille d'eau minérale.

Jer voodray ewn caraf der vang ordeenair, ay ewn bootay doe meenairall.
I would like a carafe of house wine and a bottle of mineral water.

Qu'est-ce que vous avez comme jus de fruits ?

Kessker vooz avay komm zhew der fwee?
What fruit juices have you got?

Excusez-moi, j'ai renversé mon verre.

Exkewzay mwah, jay ronvairsay mong vair.
I'm sorry, I've spilt my drink.

Nous sommes un peu pressés.

Noo somms urn per pressay.
We are in a bit of a hurry.

Problems with the bill

Qu'est-ce que cela veut dire ?

Kessker sirlah ver deer?
What does this mean?

The Menu

Café Menu

Café complet
Caffay complay
Continental breakfast

Pain grillé
Pang greeyay
Toast

Croissant
Cwassong
Crescent-shaped roll

Beurre et confiture
Burr ay konfeetyour
Butter and jam

Croque-Monsieur
Crock Moosyer
**Welsh Rarebit
with ham**

Omelette
Omlett
Omelette

Croque-Madame
Crock Madarm
**Welsh Rarebit with
ham and fried egg**

Salade mixte
Salad meext
Mixed salad

Sandwich
Sondweech
Sandwich

Quiche Lorraine
Keesh Lorrenn
Egg and bacon flan

Glaces
Glass
Ice cream

Les Consommations
Lay Consom-asseeon
Drinks

Pâtisserie
Pateessree
Pastries and cakes

Café
Caffay
Coffee (black)

Fromage
Fromarj
Cheese

Café au lait
Caffay oh lay
White coffee

Chocolat chaud
Shokolah show
Hot chocolate

Oeuf dur
Urf dyoor
Hard-boiled egg

Thé
Tay
Tea

Pommes frites
Pomm freet
Chips

Orange pressée
Oranj pressay
Fresh orange juice

28

Restaurant menu

Keep a look out for menus which advertise a special set meal, called a *Menu du Jour*, *Menu à Prix Fixe* or a *Menu Touristique*. They are cheaper than eating *A la Carte*, where you can choose anything on the menu you like.

Remember that there is usually a cover charge *(le couvert)* for each person.

La Carte

Assiette de crudités
Assee-ett der crewdeetay
Plate of raw vegetables

Les escargots
Lez escargo
Snails

Les cuisses de grenouilles
Lay cwees der grenoo-ee
Frogs legs

Les Entrées

Lez ontray
Main courses

Boeuf bourguignon
Berf boorgeenyon
Beef cooked in red wine

Selle d'agneau
Sell danyo
Saddle of lamb

Poulet à l'estragon
Poolay ah lestra-gone
Chicken in tarragon sauce

Médaillons de veau
Med-eye-ong der voe
Veal steaks

Rôti de porc
Roetee der porr
Roast pork

Canard aux cerises
Canarr oh sereez
Duck with cherries

Les Poissons

Lay pwusson
Fish

Moules
Mool
Mussels

Les crustacés
Lay kroostassay
Shell fish

Le homard
Ler ommar
Lobster

Les Légumes

Lay legyoom
Vegetables

Les Entremets

Lez ontrer-may
Puddings

Fromage

Le plateau de fromages
Ler plattoh der fromarj
Cheese board

Tarte aux pommes
Tart oh pomm
Apple tart

Crêpes
Crepp
Pancakes

Plat du jour
Plah dew joor
Today's special dish

T.V.A.
V.A.T.

Service non compris
Sairvees nong compree
Service not included

Entertainments 1

You should be able to find out what you can see from a local paper, the Tourist Office *(Syndicat d'Initiative)*, or the hotel receptionist. Smoking is forbidden in cinemas and theatres. You are expected to tip the usherette.

Qu'est-ce que vous pouvez me conseiller comme spectacle à voir?

Kessker voo poovay mer consay-yay comm specktarckl ah vwar?

Can you recommend a show to see?

Le Cirque
Ler Seerk
Circus

Théâtre de Marionnettes
Tayartr der Marry-o-nett
Puppet Theatre

Un Dessin Animé
Urn Dessang Aneemay
Cartoon Film

Théâtre en Plein Air
Tayartr ong Plen Air
Open-Air Theatre

Une Fête Foraine
Ewn Fet Foren
Fairground

Une Pièce de Théâtre
Ewn Pee-ess der Tay-attre
A Play

Son et Lumière
Song ay Lewmee-air
Sound and Light Show
(These tell the story of famous old buildings, in which they are held.)

Le Magicien
Ler Majeesee-an
Magician

Un Match de Football
Urn Match dur Football
Football Match

Qu'est-ce qu'on joue au cinéma ce soir ?

Est-ce qu'il y a un film en anglais ?

Kesskong joo oh seenaymah sir swar?
What is on at the cinema tonight?

Esskeel ya urn feelm on ong-glay?
Is there a film in English?

Quel est le prix des places ?

Deux places à l'orchestre.

Kell ay ler pree day plass?
How much are the tickets?

Durr plass ah lorkesstr.
Two seats in the stalls.

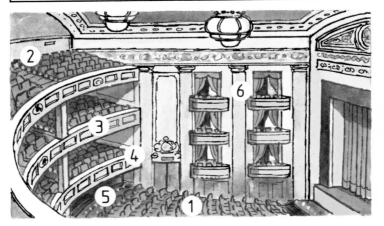

1 L'orchestre
Lorkesstr
The Stalls

2 La Galerie
Lah Galree
The Gallery

3 Le Deuxième Balcon
Ler Derzee-em Balkong
Upper Circle

4 La Corbeille
Lah Corbay
First Circle

5 Les Baignoires
Lay Baynwar
Dress Circle

6 Les Loges d'Avant-Scène
Lay Loj Davong Senn
Boxes

31

Entertainments 2

A quelle heure commence le spectacle?

A 18 heures 30. Il se termine à 20 heures.

Ah kell urr commorss ler specktarckl?
What time does the show begin?

Ah deezweet urr tront. Eel sir tairmeen ah vant urr.
At six-thirty p.m. It finishes at eight o'clock.

Où est-ce que je peux acheter un programme, s'il vous plaît?

Oo essker jer per ashtay urn program, seelvooplay?
Where can I buy a programme, please?

L'ouvreuse en vend.

Loovrerz ong von.
The usherette sells them.

Theatre signs

LE VESTIAIRE

Cloakroom

SORTIE DE SECOURS →

Fire Exit

TOILETTES

Toilets

DÉFENSE DE FUMER

No Smoking

INTERDIT AUX MOINS DE 18 ANS

INTERDIT AUX MOINS DE 13 ANS

These signs mean that children under the ages of 18 or 13 are not allowed to see the show.

This sign means that the show is a great success.

Sightseeing 1

The *Syndicat d'Initiative* or *Office de Tourisme* will also give you sightseeing information. You will usually have to pay an entrance fee to places of interest. Museums are often closed on Mondays or Tuesdays, and some places are closed in winter.

Qu'est-ce qu'il y a d'intéressant à voir dans la ville?

Kesskeel ya dantairessong ah vwar dong lah veel?
What is there of interest to see in the town?

Places to go sightseeing

Le Château
Ler Shattoh
The Castle

Le Jardin Zoologique
Ler Jardang Zo-olojeek
The Zoo

Le Musée
Ler Mewzay
The Museum

L'Église
Leggleez
The Church

Le Vieux Quartier
Ler Vyer Kartee-yay
Old Part of Town

Parc National
Park Nasseeonal
Nature Reserve

Les Grottes
Lay Grott
Caves

Est-ce qu'il y a un plan touristique de la ville?

Esskeel ya urn plong tooristeek der lah veel?
Is there a tourist map of the town?

Est-ce que vous pouvez me dire quand le musée est ouvert?

Essker voo poovay mer deer cong ler mewzay ett oovair?
Can you tell me when the museum is open?

Tous les jours sauf le mardi, de 9 heures à 18 heures.

Too lay joor sohf ler mardee, der nerf urr ah deezweet urr.
Every day except Tuesday, from 9 a.m. to 6 p.m.

Quel est le prix de l'entrée?

Kell ay ler pree der lontray?
How much is the admission charge?

Sightseeing 2

Guided tours

Y a-t-il une visite guidée en anglais ?

Ee ateel ewn vizeet geeday ong ong-glay ?
Is there a guided tour in English?

Oui. La prochaine visite commence dans un quart d'heure.

Wee. Lah proshain vizeet commonss donz urn kar durr.
Yes. The next tour starts in a quarter of an hour.

La visite prend combien de temps ?

Lah vizeet prong combeeyen der tong?
How long does the tour last?

Peut-on monter en haut de la tour ?

Pert ong montay on oh der lah toor?
Can one go up the tower?

At the zoo

Le Vivarium
Ler Veevaree-oom
Reptile House

La Volière
Lah Volee-air
The Aviary

Les Singes
Lay Sanj
Monkey House

Le Goûter des Chimpanzés
Ler Gootay day Shimpanza
Chimpanzees Tea-Party

La Fosse aux Ours
Lah Foss oh Oors
Bear Pit

Promenade à dos d'âne
Promenard ah doe dan
Donkey rides

Promenade à chameau
Promernard ah shamoh
Camel rides

Signs

Do not Feed
the Animals

Dangerous
Animals

Wild Animals

Entrance

Exit

Do not Touch

Cameras Prohibited

Tea-Room

Private Property

Beware of
the Dog

No Entrance

Closed for
the Holidays

Open

Closed

Keep off
the Grass

Making Friends

Bongjoor. Commong tappell tew ?
Hello. What is your name ?

Jer mappell Marree. Ay twa ?
My name is Mary. And yours ?

Oo pass tew lay vackonss ?
Where are you staying ?

Jabeet lah bah.
I live over there.

Kell arj ah tew ?
How old are you ?

Jay dooz ong.
I'm 12.

Oui. Ja'ai une soeur aînée, et voici mon frère jumeau.

Vwussee mong frair Jong. Ah tew day frair ay sir ?
This is my brother John. Have you any brothers and sisters ?

We. Jay ewn sir aynay, ay vwussee mong frair jewmoh.
Yes. I have an elder sister, and this is my twin brother.

36

Pouvez-vous déjeuner avec nous ?

Poovay voo dayjernay aveck noo ?
Can you have lunch with us ?

Il faut que je demande à nos parents.

Eel foe ker jer demond ah no parong.
I must ask our parents.

On va jouer.

Ong vah jooay
Let's go and play !

Dépêchez-vous !

J'arrive !

Attends-moi !

Daypeshay voo !
Hurry up !

Jarreev !
I'm coming !

Attong-mwa !
Wait for me !

J'aime . .

Jaim . .
I like . .

Jeu d'échecs
Jer daysheck
Chess

La Peinture
Lah Pantewr
Painting

La Menuiserie
Lah Menweezeree
Woodwork

La Philatélie
Lah Feelataylee
Stamp Collecting

Cards

Les Carreaux
Lay Carroh
Diamonds

Les Cœurs
Lay Curr
Hearts

Les Trèfles
Lay Treffl
Clubs

Les Piques
Lay Peek
Spades

Le Roi
Ler Rwah
King

La Reine
Lah Renn
Queen

Le Valet
Ler Vallay
Jack

L'As
Lass
Ace

Le Joker
Ler Jokair
Joker

Playing Games

39

Sports

There is a lot of good fishing in France, especially for trout, pike and salmon. For river and lake fishing, you must join an anglers' association *(une association de pêche et de pisciculture)*. To do this, ask at a fishing tackle shop.

Going fishing

Où est-ce que je peux louer une canne à pêche?

Oo essker jer per looay ewn cann ah pesh?
Where can I hire a fishing-rod?

Ça fait combien pour la journée?

Sah fay combeeyen poor lah jornày?
How much does it cost for the day?

Faut-il avoir un permis?

Foe-teel avwar urn pairmee?
Must one have a permit?

Avez-vous des appâts, s'il vous plaît?

Avay-voo dez appah, seelvooplay?
Have you any bait, please?

Est-ce un bon endroit pour pêcher?

Ess urn bong ondrwa poor peshay?
Is this a good place to fish?

Riding

Peut-on monter à cheval près d'ici?

Pert-ong montay ah sherval pray dee-see?
Can one go riding near here?

Nous voudrions prendre des cours d'équitation.

Noo voodreeong prondr day coor deckee tasseeong.
We would like some riding lessons.

40

Skiing

Les Chaussures de Ski
Lay Showsyoor der Skee
Ski Boots

Les Skis
Lay Skee
Skis

Les Bâtons de Ski
Lay Battong der Skee
Ski Sticks

Les Gants de Ski
Lay Gong der Skee
Ski Gloves

Un Abonnement
Urn Abonmong
Ski Pass

Où se trouve l'école de ski?

Oo sir troov leckoll dur skee?
Where is the ski school?

The ski runs

The ski runs, or *Pistes,* are marked with coloured arrows.

Nursery slopes-very easy.

Beginners-easy.

For quite experienced skiers-quite difficult.

For professional skiers -very difficult.

Je suis débutant.

Jer swee debewtong.
I am a beginner.

J'ai déjà skié une fois.

Jay dayja skeeay ewn fwah.
I have skied once before.

Je suis assez fort.

Jer swee assay for.
I am quite experienced.

Je ne peux pas me lever. Pouvez-vous m'aider?

Jer ner per pah mer levay. Poovay-voo mayday?
I cannot get up. Can you help me?

Nous sommes perdus. Où est le téléski?

Noo somm pairdew. Oo ay ler taylayskee?
We are lost. Where is the ski-lift?

At the Seaside 1

Où est la plage la plus proche?

Y a-t-il une piscine?

Oo ay lah plarj lah plew prosh?
Where is the nearest beach?

Ee ateel ewn pesseen?
Is there a swimming pool?

Je voudrais louer deux matelas, une chaise longue . . .

. . . et un parasol.

Jer voodray looay durr materlah, ewn shairz longg . . .
I would like to hire two mattresses, a deck chair . . .

. . . ay urn parasol.
. . . and a parasol.

Où est-ce que je peux me changer?

A côté du bassin.

Oo essker jer per mer shongjay?
Where are the changing rooms?
Ah coatay dew bassang.
Next to the paddling pool.

Beach things

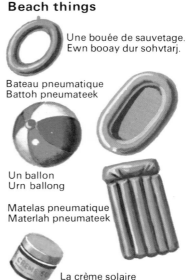

Une bouée de sauvetage.
Ewn booay dur sohvtarj.

Bateau pneumatique
Battoh pneumateek

Un ballon
Urn ballong

Matelas pneumatique
Materlah pneumateek

La crème solaire
Lah crem solair

42

Bonjour. On va se baigner?

Bongjoor. Ong vah sir baynyay?
Hello. Let's go for a swim.

Pourriez-vous vous occuper de mes affaires, s'il vous plaît?

Pooree-ay voo vooz ockewpay der mez affair, seelvooplay?
Please could you look after my .things for me?

Attention! Voilà une grosse vague!

Attongseeong! Vwullah ewn gross varg!
Watch out! There's a big wave coming!

Y a-t-il une douche?

Ee ateel ewn doosh?
Is there a shower?

Passe-moi la serviette.

Pass mwah lah sairveeyet.
Pass me the towel.

Le Ski Nautique
Ler Skee Nohteek
Water Skiing

Les Cours de Natation
Lay Coor dur Natasseeong
Swimming Lessons

Pédalos
Pedalow
Pedaloes

Voiliers
Vwullee-ay
Sailing Boats

At the Seaside 2

On construit un château de sable?

As-tu un seau et une pelle?

Ong constrwee urn shattoh dur sarbl?
Shall we build a sand castle?

Ah-tew urn soe ay ewn pell?
Have you got a bucket and spade?

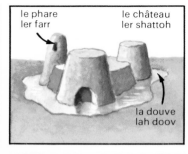

le phare
ler farr

le château
ler shattoh

la douve
lah doov

Que signifie le drapeau rouge?

Ker seenyeefee ler drapoh rooj?
What does the red flag mean?

Il est dangereux de se baigner. La mer est trop agitée.

DÉFENSE DE SE BAIGNER

Eel ay dongjay-rer der sir baynyay. Lah mair ay troh ajeetay.
It is dangerous to swim. The sea is too rough.

No Bathing

J'ai chaud.

Jay show.
I'm hot.

On va acheter une glace?

Ong vah ashtay ewn glass?
Shall we buy an ice cream?

44

Buying an ice cream

Exkewsay mwah. Avay voo day glass?
Excuse me. Do you have any ice creams?

We. Kel parfang voolay voo?
Yes. What flavour would you like?

Vanille
Vanee
Vanilla

Fraise
Frairz
Strawberry

Framboise
Frombwarz
Raspberry

Praliné
Praleenay
Nutty

Pistache
Peestash
Pistachio

Chocolat
Shok-o-lah
Chocolate

Jer voodray ewn glass ah lah vanee.
I would like a vanilla ice cream.

Ewn sampl oo ewn doobl?
A single or a double cornet?

Ewn doobl ay urn eskimo ah lah frairz.
A double and a strawberry lolly.

Sa fay combeeyen?
How much is that?

Wee frong.
Eight francs.

Mairsee.
Thank you.

45

Accidents and Emergencies

The numbers for fire, police and ambulance services are given on the central disc of the telephone (see page 48). Road accidents should be reported to the police station *(Gendarmerie)* immediately. If you are in serious trouble, contact a British Consulate.

Au secours !

Oh sircoor !
Help !

Venez vite !

Vernay vite !
Come quickly !

Au feu !

Oh furr !
Fire !

Appelez une ambulance, s'il vous plaît.

Applay ewn ombewlonss, seelvooplay.
Please call for an ambulance.

Missing persons

Mon ami est absent depuis hier soir.

Mong amee ett absong derpwee ee-air swar.
My friend has been missing since last night.

Quand l'avez-vous vu pour la dernière fois ?

Kong lavay voo vew poor lah dairneeair fwa ?
When did you last see him ?

Il est sorti à 18 heures pour acheter un journal.

Eel ay sortee ah deezweet urr poor ashtay urn joornal.
He went out at 6.00 p.m. to buy a newspaper.

Il portait une écharpe et un chapeau rouges.

Eel portay ewn esharp ay urn shappoh rooj.
He was wearing a red scarf and hat.

Lost or stolen

> J'ai perdu mon passeport.

Jay pairdew mong passporr.
I have lost my passport.

> On m'a volé mon porte feuille.

Ong mah volay mong port-foy.
My wallet has been stolen.

> On a cambriolé ma chambre.

Ong ah combree-olay mah shormbr.
My room has been burgled.

> Où pouvons-nous vous contacter ?

Oo poovong noo voo contacktay ?
Where can we contact you ?

Other things

mes chèques de voyage
may sheck dur vweye-arj
my traveller's cheques

mon appareil photo-graphique
mong apparay fotografeek
my camera

ma valise
mah valeez
my suitcase

mes clefs
may clay
my keys

mon sac
mong sack
my bag

ma montre
mah montr
my watch

> Ça s'est passé entre 10 heures et midi.

Sa say passay ontr deess urr ay meedee.
It happened between 10.00 a.m. and midday.

> Voici mon nom et mon adresse.

Vwussee mong nom ay mong address.
Here is my name and address.

47

Using the Telephone

You will find public telephones in post offices and most cafés. Some are operated by coins, others by special tokens, called jetons, which you can buy in a post office or café. There are also phones which use telephone cards, obtainable in a post office or *tabac*.

On coin-operated phones, you usually have to insert the coin before dialling. The dialling tone is a high-pitched buzz. After you have dialled, you wil hear a series of short pips while the line is connecting. Then you will hear the ringing tone – a long buzz followed by a short pause.

On *jeton*-operated phones, do not put the token in until someone answers.

The telephone dial

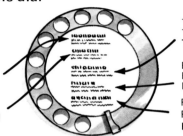

This is what the names in the centre of the dial mean.

Renseignements
Ronsaynyemong
Enquiries

Réclamations
Rayclamasseeong
Out of Order

Télégraphe
Taylay graf
Telegrams

Police-Secours
Poleess-Sekoor
Police

Pompiers
Pompeeyay
Fire Brigade

Est-ce que je peux me servir du téléphone, s'il vous plaît?

Essker jer per mer sairveer dew taylayfone, seelvooplay?
Please may I use the telephone?

Making a phone call

Je voudrais appeler Londres en P.C.V. Le numéro est 800 6009 à Londres.

Jer voodray zapplay Londr ong Pay Say Vay. Ler newmairo ay weet song, swussont, zairo, nerf ah Londr.
I want to call London and reverse the charges. The number is London 800 6009.

Puis-je avoir trois jetons, s'il vous plaît?

Pwee javwar twah jurtong, seelvooplay?
Please may I have three telephone tokens?

Quel est votre numéro ?
Ne quittez pas.

Kell ay vottr newmairo ? Ner keetay pah.
What is your number ? Hold the line.

Vous vous êtes trompé de numéro.

Voo vooz ett trompay der newmairo.
You have the wrong number.

Est-ce que je pourrais parler à M. Dupont, s'il vous plaît ?

Essker jer per parlay ah Moosyer Dewpong, seelvooplay ?
Please may I speak to Mr Dupont ?

Le numéro est occupé.

Ler newmairo ett ockewpay.
The number is engaged.

Il n'est pas ici en ce moment.

C'est de la part de qui ?

Eel nay paz ee-see ong sir momong.
He is not here at the moment.

Say dur lah par dur kee ?
Who is speaking ?

Pourriez-vous lui dire que Mme Brown a téléphoné, et lui demander de m'appeler à ce numéro.

Pooree-ay voo lwee deer ker Madamm Brown a taylayfonay, ay lwee demongday der mapplay ah sir newmairo.
Could you tell him that Mrs Brown telephoned, and ask him to ring me at this number

Feeling Ill

The *pharmacie* will be able to give you advice and medicine for most minor ailments. If you see a doctor, you will have to pay him on the spot. Residents of E.E.C. countries can get most of their money refunded, when they get home, if they have to pay for hospital treatment.

J'ai mal à la tête.
Jay mal ah lah tet.
I have a headache.

J'ai mal au ventre.
Jay mal oh vorntr.
I have a stomach pain.

Je suis enrhumé.
Jer sweez onrewmay.
I have a cold.

Je tousse énormément.
Jer tooss aynormaymong.
I am coughing a lot.

J'ai de la fièvre.
Jay dur lah fee-airvr.
I have a temperature.

J'ai mal au cœur.
Jay mal oh curr.
I feel sick.

Je me suis coupé.
Jer mer swee coopay
I have cut myself.

Je me suis brûlé.
Jer mer swee brewlay.
I have burnt myself.

J'ai attrapé un coup de soleil.
Jay attrapay urn coo der solay.
I am sunburnt.

Je me suis fait piquer par . . .
Jer mer swee fay peekay par . . .
I have been stung (or bitten) by . . .

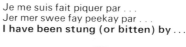

. . . une méduse.
. . . ewn medewz
. . . **a jellyfish.**

. . . un oursin.
. . . urn oorsang.
. . . **a sea-urchin.**

. . . un serpent.
. . . urn sairpong.
. . . **a snake.**

. . une guêpe.
. . . ewn gepp.
. . . **a wasp.**

J'ai quelque chose
dans l'œil.
Jay kellker showz
dong loy.
**I have something in
my eye.**

J'ai une éruption.
Jay ewn eroopsseeong.
I have a rash.

Ça me gratte.
Sa mer gratt.
It itches.

J'ai mal aux dents.
Jay mal oh dong.
I have toothache.

J'ai été attaqué par un
chien.
Jay ettay attackay par
urn shee-en.
**I have been attacked
by a dog.**

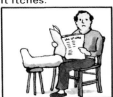

Je me suis cassé la
jambe.
Jer mer swee cassay
lah jomb.
I have broken my leg.

Going to the doctor

Il me faut voir un
médecin.

Eel mer foe vwar urn medsang.
I need to see a doctor.

Quand est-il libre?

Kont est eel leebr?
When is he free?

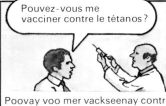

Pouvez-vous me
vacciner contre le tétanos?

Poovay voo mer vackseenay contr
ler tetanos?
**Can you inoculate me against
tetanus?**

Pouvez-vous me donner
une ordonnance?

Poovay-voo mer donnay ewn
ordononss?
Can you give me a prescription?

Parts of the Body

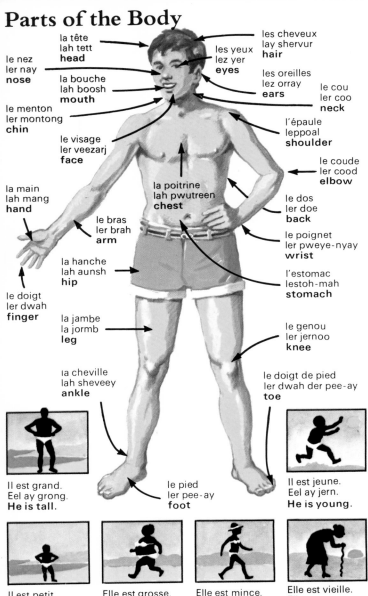

les cheveux
lay shervur
hair

la tête
lah tett
head

les yeux
lez yer
eyes

le nez
ler nay
nose

la bouche
lah boosh
mouth

les oreilles
lez orray
ears

le cou
ler coo
neck

le menton
ler montong
chin

l'épaule
leppoal
shoulder

le visage
ler veezarj
face

le coude
ler cood
elbow

la main
lah mang
hand

la poitrine
lah pwutreen
chest

le dos
ler doe
back

le bras
ler brah
arm

le poignet
ler pweye-nyay
wrist

la hanche
lah aunsh
hip

l'estomac
lestoh-mah
stomach

le doigt
ler dwah
finger

la jambe
la jormb
leg

le genou
ler jernoo
knee

la cheville
lah sheveey
ankle

le doigt de pied
ler dwah der pee-ay
toe

Il est grand.
Eel ay grong.
He is tall.

le pied
ler pee-ay
foot

Il est jeune.
Eel ay jern.
He is young.

Il est petit.
Eel ay pertee.
He is short.

Elle est grosse.
Ell ay gross.
She is fat.

Elle est mince.
Ell ay manse.
She is thin.

Elle est vieille.
Ell ay veeay.
She is old.

52

Colours
Les Couleurs (Lay Coolurr)

noir
nwar
black

blanc
blong
white

gris
gree
grey

beige
bairj
beige

brun
bruh
brown

jaune
joan
yellow

orange
oronj
orange

rouge
rooj
red

rose
roz
pink

violet
vee-olay
violet

bleu
bler
blue

vert
vair
green

or
or
gold

argent
arjong
silver

foncé
fonsay
dark

clair
clair
light

Months, Seasons and Days

Janvier
Jonveeyay
January

Février
Fevreeyay
February

Mars
Marss
March

Avril
Avreel
April

Mai
May
May

Juin
Jwang
June

Juillet
Jweeyay
July

Août
Oot
August

Septembre
Septombr
September

Octobre
Ocktobr
October

Novembre
Novombr
November

Décembre
Dayssombr
December

La Semaine (Lah Sirmen)

7 Lundi
Lurndee
Monday

8 Mardi
Mardee
Tuesday

9 Mercredi
Mairkrerdee
Wednesday

Déjeuner avec Jean

10 Jeudi
Jerdee
Thursday

11 Vendredi
Vondrerdee
Friday

12 Samedi
Samdee
Saturday

Dentiste

13 Dimanche
Deemonsh
Sunday

Les Saisons (Lay Sezong)

Le Printemps
Ler Prantong
The Spring

L'été
Lettay
The Summer

L'automne
Lohtonn
The Autumn

L'hiver
Leevair
The Winter

The Weather

**Le Temps
(Ler Tong)**

Il pleut.
Eel pler.
It's raining.

Il va pleuvoir.
Eel vah plervwar.
It's going to rain.

La grêle
Lah grell
Hail

Il y a du vent.
Eel ya dew vong.
It's windy.

Il neige.
Eel nairj.
It's snowing.

Il y a des nuages.
Eel ya day newarj.
It's cloudy.

Le tonnerre
Ler tonnair
Thunder

Un éclair
Urn ecklair
A flash of lightning.

Quel orage!
Kell orarj
What a storm!

Il fait beau.
Eel fay boe.
It's a nice day.

Il fait chaud.
Eel fay show.
It is hot.

Il fait froid.
Eel fay frwah.
It is cold.

Numbers

1	un urn	**20**	vingt vang	**73**	soixante-treize swussont-trairz
2	deux durr	**21**	vingt-et-un vantayurn	**74**	soixante-quatorze swussont-kattorz
3	trois trwa	**22**	vingt-deux vandurr	**75**	soixante-quinze swussont-kanz
4	quatre kattr	**23**	vingt-trois vantrwa	**76**	soixante-seize swussont-sairz
5	cinq sank	**24**	vingt-quatre vankattr	**77**	soixante-dix-sept swussont-deesset
6	six seess	**25**	vingt-cinq vansank	**78**	soixante-dix-huit swussont-deezweet
7	sept set	**26**	vingt-six vantseess	**79**	soixante-dix-neuf swussont-deeznerf
8	huit weet	**27**	vingt-sept vantset	**80**	quatre-vingts kattr-vang
9	neuf nerf	**28**	vingt-huit vantweet	**81**	quatre-vingt-un kattr-vang-urn
10	dix deess	**29**	vingt-neuf vantnerf	**82**	quatre-vingt-deux kattr-vang-durr
11	onze orz	**30**	trente tront	**90**	quatre-vingt-dix kattr-vang-deess
12	douze dooz	**31**	trente et un tront ay urn	**91**	quatre-vingt-onze kattr-vangorz
13	treize trairz	**32**	trente-deux trontdurr	**92**	quatre-vingt-douze kattr-vang-dooz
14	quatorze kattorz	**40**	quarante karront	**100**	cent song
15	quinze kanz	**50**	cinquante sankont	**150**	cent cinquante song sankont
16	seize sairz	**60**	soixante swussont	**1,000**	mille meel
17	dix-sept deeset	**70**	soixante-dix swussont-deess	**1,000,000**	un million urn meeleeong
18	dix-huit deezweet	**71**	soixante et onze swussont ay onz	**1st**	premier prermeeay
19	dix-neuf deeznerf	**72**	soixante-douze swussont-dooz	**2nd**	deuxième derzee-em

The Time

Officially the 24 hour clock is used in France, so times after midday are written as 13.00, 14.00 and so on. Another point to remember is that the French say, for example, "six hours less five minutes", instead of "five minutes to six" like we do.

Quelle heure est-il, s'il vous plaît?

Kell urr etteel, sealvooplay?
What time is it please?

Il est huit heures.
Eel ay weet urr.
It is eight o'clock.

Il est huit heures et quart.
Eel ay weet urr ay karr.
It is quarter past eight.

Il est neuf heures moins le quart.
Eel ay nerf urr mwang ler karr.
It is quarter to nine.

Il est midi.
Eel ay meedee.
It is midday.

Il est sept heures moins cinq.
Eel ay sank urr mwang sank.
It is five to seven.

Il est sept heures dix.
Eel ay set urr deess.
It is ten past seven.

Il est dix heures et demie.
Eel ay deess urr ay dermee.
It is half past ten.

Il est minuit.
Eel ay meenwee.
It is midnight.

le matin
ler matang
the morning

l'après-midi
lappray meedee
the afternoon

le soir
ler swar
the evening

la nuit
lah nwee
the night

Time phrases

hier ee-air **yesterday**	cette année set annay **this year**	de bonne heure der bonn urr **early**	dans cinq minutes dong sank minewt **in five minutes**
aujourd'hui ohjoordwee **today**	le mois dernier ler mwah dairnee-ay **last month**	plus tôt plew toe **earlier**	dans un quart d'heure donz karr durr **in a quarter of**
demain dermang **tomorrow**	la semaine prochaine ah simen proshain **next week**	bientôt bee-entoe **soon**	**an hour**
avant-hier avont-ee-air **the day before yesterday**		plus tard plew tar **later**	dans une demi- heure donz ewn dermee urr **in half an hour**
le lendemain ler londermang **the following day**	maintenant manthong **now**	jamais jamay **never**	dans une heure' donz ewn urr **in an hour**

59

Basic Grammar

Nouns

All French nouns are either masculine or feminine. When you learn a noun, you must learn this as well. The word for "the" is *le* before masculine(m) nouns and *la* before feminine(f) nouns,

e.g. *le chien* (the dog)
la maison (the house).

If *le* or *la* comes before a noun beginning with a,e,i,o,u or h (with some exceptions), it becomes *l'*, e.g. *l'arbre* (the tree).

If the noun is plural (p), the word for "the" is *les*,
e.g. *les chiens* (the dogs)
les maisons (the houses)
les arbres (the trees).
In the plural, most French nouns have "s" on the end.

The French for "a" or "an" is *un* before masculine nouns and *une* before feminine nouns.
e.g. *un chien* (a dog)
une maison (a house).

This, that

The French use the same word for "this" and "that". It is *ce* before masculine nouns and *cette* before feminine nouns. If *ce* comes before a noun beginning with a,e,i,o or u, it becomes *cet*. The word for "these" or "those" is *ces*.

e.g. *ce chien*   (this dog)
cette maison (this house)
cet arbre   (this tree)
ces chiens   (these dogs)
ces maisons (these houses)
ces arbres   (these trees)

Pronouns

The French word for "it" or "they" depends on whether the noun it replaces is masculine or feminine,
e.g. *le chien mange* (the dog eats)
il mange   (it eats)

I	je
you	tu
he, it (m)	il
she, it (f)	elle
we	nous
you (p)	vous
they (m)	ils
they (f)	elles

Possessive adjectives

The word you use for "my", "your", "his" etc. depends on whether the word that follows it is masculine, feminine or plural,

e.g. *mon chien* (m) (my dog)
sa maison (f) (his or her house)
tes frères (p) (your brothers)

	(m)	(f)	(p)
my	mon	ma	mes
your	ton	ta	tes
his, hers, its	son	sa	ses
our	notre	notre	nos
your (p)	votre	votre	vos
their	leur	leur	leurs

Useful verbs

avoir	to have
j'ai	I have
tu as	you have
il a	he/it has
elle a	she/it has
nous avons	we have
vous avez	you have (p)
ils ont	they have (m)
elles ont	they have (f)

être	to be
je suis	I am
tu es	you are
il est	he/it is
elle est	she/it is
nous sommes	we are
vous êtes	you are (p)
ils sont	they are (m)
elles sont	they are (f)

parler	to speak
je parle	I speak
tu parles	you speak
il parle	he/it speaks
elle parle	she/it speaks
nous parlons	we speak
vous parlez	you speak (p)
ils parlent	they speak (m)
elles parlent	they speak (f)

venir	to come
je viens	I come
tu viens	you come
il vient	he/it comes
elle vient	she/it comes
nous venons	we come
vous venez	you come (p)
ils viennent	they come (m)
elles viennent	they come (f)

aller	to go
je vais	I go
tu vas	you go
il va	he/it goes
elle va	she/it goes
nous allons	we go
vous allez	you go (p)
ils vont	they go (m)
elles vont	they go (f)

vouloir	to want
je veux	I want
tu veux	you want
il veut	he/it wants
elle veut	she/it wants
nous voulons	we want
vous voulez	you want (p)
ils veulent	they want (m)
elles veulent	they want (f)

Negatives

To make a verb negative, add *ne* before the verb and *pas* after it. If *ne* comes before a vowel, it becomes *n'*,

e.g. je parle français   I speak French
je ne parle pas français   I do not speak French
j'ai   I have
je n'ai pas   I have not

Questions.....

There are two ways you can ask a question in French. You can either put the verb before the pronoun, or you can use the phrase *est-ce que* at the beginning of the question,

e.g. *vous voulez*   you want
voulez-vous?   do you want?
est-ce que vous voulez?   do you want?

Index

This index lists some words individually and some under group names, such as food. Where you will find the French for the indexed word, the page number is printed in italics, like this: *6*.

accidents, 46, 50, 51
afternoon, *59*
age, 36
air mail, *23*
airport, *7*
ambulance, *46*
antiseptic cream, *21*
aspirin, *21*

bandage, *21*
bank, *7*
bank, opening hours, 23
bathroom, *12*
battery (car), *21*
beach, *42*
bicycling, *39*
big, *17*
bill,
    café, 25
    hotel, 13
biscuits, *18*
bites and stings, 50
body, parts of the, 52
book, *20*
booking,
    hotel, 12
    restaurant table, 26
    theatre, 31
bookshop, *20*
bread, *19*
breakdown, 10
breakfast, *13*, 28
brother, *36*
burglary, 47
burns, 50
bus, *6*
bus-stop, *6*
butcher, *19*
butter, *18*

cafés, 24–5, 48
cakes, *19*, 28
camera, *47*
cameras prohibited, *35*
camping, 14–15
camping gas, *21*

camping signs, 15
car, 10–11
cards, 37
car hire, 10
castle, *6*, *33*
caves, *33*
changing money, 23
cheese, *18*, *28*, *29*
chemist, *21*, *50*
church, *33*
cinema, 30, *31*
circus, *30*
cloakroom, *32*
closed, *35*
clothes, 17, 20
coffee, *18*, *28*
cold, *56*
colours, 53
comb, *21*
corkscrew, *21*
cotton (thread), *21*
cuts, 50

days, 55
deck chair, *42*
detergent, *21*
dial, telephone, 48
dinner, *13*
directions, 6–7
doctor, 50, *51*
drinks, 24, 27, *28*

early, *59*
eating, 24–5, 26–7,
    28–9
eggs, *13*, *18*, *28*
emergencies, 46–7
entertainments, 30–1,
    32
entrance, *35*
envelopes, *20*
evening, *59*
exit, *35*

fairground, *30*
film (cinema), *31*
film (photographic), *21*
fire, *46*
fire brigade, *48*
fire exit, *32*
fish, 19, *29*
fishing, 40
food, 16, 18–19, 24,
    26–7, 28–9
football, *30*
fork, *25*
friends, 36
frogs' legs, *29*
fruit, *16*, 18

games, 37, 38–9
garage, *10*
glass, *25*
grocer, *18*
groceries, 18
guided tour, *34*

handbag, *47*
hardware store, *21*
headache, *50*
help, *46*
hobbies, 37
honey, *18*
hospital, 50
hot, *44*, *56*
hotel,
    bill, *13*
    booking, 12
    keys, *13*
    meals, 13
    room, *12*
how much, 17

icecream, *28*, 44–5
illness, 50–1
ink, 20
insect repellent, *21*
international calls, 48
ironmongers, *21*

jam, *18*

keys, *13*, *47*
knife, *25*

later, *59*
left luggage, *9*
letter (posting) 22
lifts, *16*
light bulb, *21*
lighter, *20*
loose, *17*
lost, *41*, *47*
lost property, *9*
lunch, 13, *37*

map, *6*, *33*
matches, *20*
mattress, beach, *42*
meals, hotel, 13
meat, 19, *29*
menu, 24, 26, 28–9
message, *13*
midday, *58*
midnight, *59*
milk, *18*
mineral water, *27*
missing persons, 46
money, changing, 23
months, 54

morning, *59*
museum, *33*
mustard, *18*

name, *36*
napkin, *25*
nature reserve, *33*
needle, *21*
never, *59*
newspapers, *20*
night, *59*
now, *59*
numbers, 57

old part of town, *33*
open, *35*
opening hours,
    banks, *23*
    shops, 16
ordering food, 24

packed lunch, *13*
paddling pool, *42*
parasol, *42*
parcels, *23*
parents, *37*
passport, 12, *47*
paying, 17, 25, 31, 45
pen, *20*
pencil, *20*
pepper, *25*
petrol, *10*
phone calls, 48–9
platform, railway, *8*
playing, 36–7, 38–9
plug, electric, *21*
police, 46, *48*
police station, *7, 46*
pork butcher, *19*
post box, *22*
post office, 22, 23, 48
post office signs, 23
prescription, *51*
programme, theatre, *32*

railway station, *7,* 8–9
restaurant, 26
riding, *40*
road signs, 11
rubber, *20*

sailing boats, *43*
sale, *16*
salt, *25*
sandwich, *24, 28*
scissors, *21*
screwdriver, *21*
sea, *44*
seaside, 42–3, 44–5

seasons, 55
self-service, *16*
service, 25, 29
shopping, 16–17
shops, 7, 18–19, 20–1
shop signs, 16
shower, *43*
sightseeing, 33, 34
signs, 9, 11, 15, 16, 23,
    32, 35
sisters, *36*
size, of clothes, *17*
skiing, 41
small, *17*
small change, *23*
snails, *29*
soap, *21*
soft drinks, 24, *27,* 28
soon, *59*
spoon, *25*
sports, 40–1, *43*
stamps, 20, 22, 23
stationers, *20*
station signs, 9
sticking plasters, *21*
stings, 50
stolen, *47*
stomach pain, *50*
sugar, *18*
suitcase, *47*
sunburn, *50*
suntan cream, *42*
sweets, *19*
swimming, 43
swimming lessons, *43*
swimming pool, *42*

tea, *18, 28*
tea-room, *35*
telegrams, *22, 23,* 48
telephone, 48–9
telephone tokens, *23,*
    48
temperature, *50*
theatre, *30,* 31
theatre signs, 32
ticket,
    railway, *8*
    theatre, *31*
ticket office, railway, *8*
tight, *17*
time phrases, 59
time, telling the, 58
tin opener, *21*
today, *59*
toilets, *25, 32*
toilet paper, *21*
tomorrow, *59*

toothache, *51*
toothbrush, *21*
toothpaste, *21*
torch, *15, 21*
tourist office, *12, 30, 33*
tours, guided, 34
towel, *43*
trains, 8–9
traveller's cheques,
    23, 47

usherette, *32*

vegetables, 18, *29*

waiter, 25
waiting room, *9*
wallet, *47*
watch, *47*
water, *9, 15*
water, jug of, *25*
water skiing, *43*
weather, 56
wine, *27*
writing paper, *20*

yesterday, *59*

zoo, *33,* 34

Index of French words

This index lists some of the French words you might see on signs and notices. Look up the page reference to find out what they mean.

aéroport, 7
à la carte, 29
ascenseur, 16

banque, 7
billets, 8
boucherie, 19
boulangerie, 19
boutique de
    vêtements, 20
brasserie, 26
bureau de change, 23

café complet, 28
caisse, 17
centre ville, 11
charcuterie, 19
château, 33
chien méchant, 35
cirque, 30
consigne, 9
consommations, 28
Croque-Madame, 28
Croque-Monsieur, 28
couvert, 29

défense de se
    baigner, 44
défense de fumer, 32
défense de nourrir les
    animaux, 35
défense de toucher, 35
dessin animé, 30
disque obligatoire, 11

eau non potable, 9
eau potable, 15
église, 33
entrée, 35
entrée interdite, 35
entrées, 29
entremets, 29
épicerie-
    alimentation, 18

fermé, 35
fermeture annuelle, 35
fête foraine, 30

gare, 7
gendarmerie, 46
glaces, 45
grottes, 33

jardin zoologique, 33
jeton, 23, 48

légumes, 29
librairie, 20
libre service, 16
livraison des bagages, 9

magicien, 30
maison de la presse, 20
médecin, 51
menu à prix fixe, 29
menu du jour, 29
menu touristique, 29
musée, 33

office de tourisme, 33
ouvert, 16, 35

papeterie, 20
paquets, 23
par avion, 23
parc national, 33

pâtisserie-confiserie, 19
péage, 11
pétanque, 38
pharmacie, 21
piscine, 42
plat du jour, 29
poissonnerie, 19
police-secours, 48
pompiers, 48
propriété privée, 35
P. & T., 22

quincaillerie, 21

réclamations, 48
relais routiers, 26
renseignements, 9, 48

salle d'attente, 9
salon de thé, 35
service non compris, 29
ski nautique, 43
soldes, 16
son et lumière, 30
sortie, 35
sortie de secours, 32
syndicat d'initiative,
    12, 30, 33

tabac, 20
tarif, 13
télégrammes, 22, 23
théâtre de
    marionnettes, 30
théâtre en plein air, 30
timbres poste, 23
toilettes, 32
toutes directions, 11

vestiaire, 32
vieux quartier, 33
voitures de location, 10